*Hannah **Arendt**'s Little Theater*

For Manolin and Félix,
because the children who disturb the work
are the ones who appreciate its meaning and worth.
M. M.-C.

To Nanou and Jacques.
C. P.

Hannah Arendt's Little Theater

Narrated by
Marion Muller-Colard

Illustrated by
Clémence Pollet

Translated by
Anna Street

Plato & Co.
diaphanes

Hannah is a palindrome. You can read it forwards and backwards.
From left to right and from right to left, it still reads Hannah.
Naturally, Hannah Arendt knew all about this. But she never
knew it better than on December 4, 1975, one very cold day.

On that particular morning, Hannah Arendt is determined
to come to terms with *The Life of the Mind*. Bent over the sink,
she splashes her face with water to refresh her ideas:
"When will I write the last word of this book? It is perhaps
my first book of philosophy," remarks the elderly lady as she
smiles mischievously at herself in the mirror. Yet...

Hannah Arendt reaches out her hand incredulously towards
the mirror: "Who are you?" murmurs the old lady to the little girl
who has appeared next to her. "I have the feeling I know you..."
From the other side of the mirror, the young girl with the long
dark braids traces H-A-N-N-A-H on the glass with her finger.

While tracing the final H, the image of the girl fades away.
Hannah Arendt lets out a heavy sigh, turns the water on,
and splashes her face again. Strange vision… Most likely,
her dreams had followed her from her bed into the bathroom.

But when she tries to begin her work, she notices a silhouette
with long dark braids sitting at her desk: "Oh my, what are
you doing here?" exclaims Hannah Arendt, crossing her arms.
"What exactly is it you want from me?"
Today, Hannah Arendt turns sixty-nine. Having never had
children, she is not used to being disturbed while she works.
"I have a book to write, young lady."
"A book? Tell me the story," begs the little girl as she clutches
an old stuffed fox with faded fur tightly to her breast.
"It isn't a story book, it's a book about… about the meaning
of words," replies Hannah, in order to cut the conversation
short.
"So do you invent words?"

7

"Invent words," broods Hannah Arendt as she paces, annoyed,
around her desk.
"They will say what they want about me, but I am anything
but someone who invents words! I am a practical thinker,
not a theoretical thinker! I do my thinking on the ground,
not under it!"

The little girl gets up from the desk and takes a seat on the floor.

"If I ignore her," muses the old lady, "perhaps she will end up
disappearing again."
But this child is a hard one to ignore. Pretty soon, she starts
speaking to herself:
"It might be the story of a fox who crawls up out of his
burrow..."
Hannah Arendt starts to lose her patience. At her typewriter,
words no longer seem to obey her.
"Or rather the story of a fox afraid of the Big Bad Wolf..."
continues the child loudly.

But after a while, she lets her little fox slip to the floor
and heaves a deep sigh:
"You see, I'm no good at it. Please, tell me a story…"
"Stubborn," observes Hannah as she continues to ignore her.

The little girl gets up and takes a look at the black letters
which appear as the typewriter is tapping away.
"If you type all that on your typewriter, then it means
you are indeed inventing words…"

One can easily imagine that for Hannah Arendt this was
the last straw.

In the streets of Manhattan, the older Hannah, exasperated,
walks briskly on, dragging the child behind her. The little girl
allows herself to be swept along. Her dark eyes are open
so wide that one could think she wants to drink in the
whole world.
"Where are you taking me?" she finally asks.
"To a theater. Telling must be acting. To tell for the sake
of telling is nothing more than to babble or to lie."

The two Hannahs walk across a large room full of empty seats.
The older Hannah climbs onto the stage. In front of them the
heavy curtain is drawn. She pushes open a crack in the folds
and slips through.

"And so, let's get going then," announces the older Hannah to
the young girl who is also making her way through the curtain.
"A story…"
"It takes people to make a story…"
"And it takes a story to make the world."
"Characters."
"Of course! If I am alone in the world, the story is too
predictable. It's because there are a number of us
that the world is what it is."

"So you don't know the en**d,** then?" asks the girl
as she tosses her toy fox in**to** the air.

And here the fox lands, all **atremble,** on his paws.
Terrified, the animal takes **refuge** under his young
owner's skirts.
"Look, my fox has come ali**ve!**" the girl squeals,
while the animal casts about **frightened** looks.

Some kind of commotion see**ms** to be arising in the wings.
The two Hannahs turn their **attention** to the tall,
dark curtains that have begu**n** **to** quiver. In the shadows,
new characters await their entrance onto the stage.

The older Hannah holds a staff out to the girl, the theater baton used to strike the customary twelve blows. But the child knits her eyebrows.

"Why is there so much noise on the other side of the red curtain?" she murmurs as she makes her way to the front of the stage.

From the other side of the curtain, the child discovers
hundreds of eyes fixed on her. She takes a step back, terrified.
"Oh dear! The young miss is panicking because she has
discovered an audience!" comments the elder Hannah.

Upset, the child takes refuge in the wings, crying.
By Jove, how sensitive a child can be...

"This story, it should be between you and me,
just for the two of us!" the girl gasps in between hiccups.

"A story worth telling is a story with spectators to judge it."

But the girl is nonetheless far from ready to come out of hiding.
So the older Hannah pretends to sulk in turn.
"If you stay in the wings to tell your own little story,
I am not interested!"

It makes one wonder which of the two Hannahs
is the more stubborn.

The girl, defeated, comes back on to the stage.
The older Hannah hands her the baton:
"It's up to you to strike the twelve blows, isn't it?"
The child feels her stomach tie up in knots.
The older Hannah encourages her:
"You were not born only to give life to your body.
You were also born..."
"For the life of the mind!" continues the girl
who remembers the book the older Hannah
is in the middle of writing.
"To think, to will, to judge...
And to take your place on stage!"

Driven by curiosity, the girl strikes eleven blows
on the floor. On the twelfth blow, the curtain
rises.

The child turns to look, dumbfounded by the scenery that has come up behind her. Tall stone columns loom at the four corners of the stage.

An old man wearing a white toga comes up to her slowly and holds out his hand.
"Aristotle, my old friend," exclaims the adult Hannah.
"My dear little Hannah, Aristotle invites you into the Agora, the public space of his antique City... an offer that cannot be turned down!"

And so the child takes the outstretched hand. Yet she is suddenly alarmed by a strange growling noise... From the wings shine two large, threatening eyes.
"What is that?" the girl asks while hiding behind the folds of the older Hannah's skirt. "It looks like the eyes of the Big Bad Wolf!"

Aristotle replies: "We, the sages of Ancient Greece, have decided to safeguard our public space against all need, all violence and all domination. This is why the Agora stretches out all around you! In order for us to exchange goods and ideas as a free people, we keep the wolf in the wings, in our private spaces."
"And is the Agora the stage for your politics?" asks the child.
"You understand perfectly," smiles the old man.

The young Hannah is somewhat reassured. The stage is empty, she can play! She lifts one side of her skirt to motion to the fox: "You can come out now, we are in the Agora and the wolf is not!"
"Leave me alone, I'm agoraphobic," retorts the fox as he pulls the skirt folds back down to hide himself.

The older Hannah smiles. "I know this old fox…
He's the kind of philosopher who doesn't like politics."
"Does agoraphobic mean one doesn't like politics?"
"In a way. Because the Agora is the heart of the Polis,
the Greek city where people govern over the world's affairs."

The child glances over at the center of the stage. Aristotle is speaking with other men. They must have trade or diplomatic projects with a neighboring country… How boring!
"Talk about a story…"

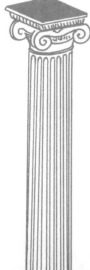

Suddenly, men loaded with boxes exit the wings and come towards the center-stage. The young Hannah follows them, intrigued. "What are you doing with all these boxes?" she asks one of them. "We're moving. We're setting up houses in the middle of the City." "But Aristotle said that the stage was the City, and the wings were the private space. You're mixing everything up!" "One has to adapt to the times, my child…"

The girl looks for the older Hannah to warn her.

Dense and spectacularly rapidly-growing ivy covers the columns
rising to the ceiling. Here and there, men are beginning new
constructions.

Finally, the child finds the older Hannah who remarks,
"It seems that people are looking for a new model. A model
in which a few take on the responsibility of public and
private affairs."
 "But then the Agora is no longer the Agora!" objects the
young Hannah.
"Exactly. Look at our friend Aristotle..."

In the middle of the stage, the old man stands transfixed.

Aristotle, rooted to the spot, still manages to call attention to the new constructions: "You are mixing up the private space behind the scenes with the public area of the stage! There will be no one left available for the task of thinking if everyone must take care of daily needs ..."

Then a crowd emerges from the wings, surging together as though a single entity with raised fists: "Equal rights for all, equal rights for all!" "These are the slaves," "explains the older to the younger Hannah. "They are the ones who took care of the needs of each household so that their masters could enjoy the liberty of the City."

Astounded, the younger Hannah watches the men parade past: "Is it a revolution?"
"Sort of. On the political scene, the revolution must be the opportunity for a new beginning."

"Look at how beautiful the new homes are!" says the younger Hannah, clapping her hands at the sight of the new city being built under their very eyes. "They are different," the older Hannah replies prudently.

But the men start to argue. One of them says that he works more than his neighbor. Another says that he doesn't have as much to eat as the others. Yet another demands perfect equality of the area between the houses that are crowding the space... And from the wings, two large eyes suddenly start to gleam.

Taking advantage of the general confusion, the wolf springs from the wings and begins to prowl around the center of the City. The younger Hannah shudders! And to think that she had begun to forget the terrifying animal...

"And who will tame the wolf?" worries the child.

A man steps forward and, with a clear voice,
makes the following proposition:
"We shall select governors from among ourselves,
and they will keep the wolf on a leash.
They will find the appropriate laws and guarantee our rights."

Aristotle, now entirely transformed into a statue,
feels his body of stone start to crumble.

In the center-stage, the newly-formed society comes together to
elect its governor. Aristotle did not know that one single person
could be thus acclaimed. In a barely-audible voice, the old man
repeats the words spoken to him by an even older sage:

Power will reveal one's true character.

Suddenly, the floor begins to tremble. Then, with a deafening roar, the buildings crack and collapse in a mass of fallen rocks. The new society disperses in a multitude of scattered individuals. Those who, earlier, created and built together, now wander about like lonely ghosts.

The older Hannah takes the younger Hannah's hand
and pulls her to the back of the stage. On the way,
the girl turns around, horrified:
"Aristotle!" she cries, in the hope of saving the old man.
"Don't worry about him!" reassures the older Hannah.
"History has made of him a free man of the City.
He will remain like that forever."

As they look about them, the two Hannahs measure
the extent of the damage: the stage is nothing more than
ruins and rubble, amid which trees have begun to grow.

Very quickly, both Hannahs find themselves imprisoned
in a thick forest of gigantic trees.

"What if the governor of the new society, instead of taming
the wolf, had let him run loose? It wouldn't be surprising
then that the City became a forest," muses the young Hannah
with a shudder.

"It is so dark! Is this the end of the story?"

"Let's find the stage of human affairs, and the story
will continue."

"Good luck, my friends!" pipes a pointy little muzzle
sticking out from the girl's skirt folds. "In my opinion,
history is setting a trap for us. As for myself, I prefer
to dig my own burrow."
And the fox flees deep into the forest.

The older Hannah sighs: "History does set traps," she admits, "but our friend the fox will one day discover the trap of the burrow."

"Nevertheless, I am scared," confesses the young Hannah with a timid voice. "I preferred the Agora... didn't you?"

"I am never nostalgic about the past. I am nostalgic about the infinite possibility of beginning."

From deep within, a light dawns in the young girl's fretful eyes.

With determined steps, the two Hannahs thread their way through the trees, which seem to want to seal off all possibility of a path before them.

"How do you expect to find the stage of human affairs in the middle of this forest?" sighs the girl as she pushes her way through the heavy foliage.

Suddenly, the girl finds herself face to face with the wolf.
He comments on his sudden appearance with an eerie calm:
"I took advantage of the general panic to slip through
the crack in the stage curtain."
The animal offhandedly picks his teeth. "Don't I have the
right to become my own master as well, charming child?"
"That remains to be seen," objects the older Hannah
just as calmly.
Yet the wolf, not the least intimidated,
comes dangerously closer.

The older Hannah stares him straight in the eyes.
"Since you left the wings to come onto the stage, you must know that laws exist. You shall not kill, for example. One of humanity's most ancient laws."
"And what if the laws change?" retorts the wolf as he comes another step closer.

This is when a small, underground voice is heard:
"Psst! You'd be better off if you joined me in my burrow!"
The girl notices the entrance to a tunnel not far away. In a few seconds, she disappears inside it. The older Hannah abandons her confrontation with the wolf in order to follow her protégé.
"Run then," the wolf cries behind them. "Run before your laws go up in smoke!"

And so both Hannahs end up in the burrow. They find the old fox in the middle of meditating. He opens only one eye, determined not to let himself be unduly interrupted by their presence:
"Make yourselves at home, ladies! You'll find everything you need to make tea..."
"That is very kind, my dear fox, but we have no intention of settling in down here."
"You mean to return to the unrest of the outside?" groans the fox with a touch of disdain.

The young Hannah, still frightened by the wolf's appearance, begs the older to accept the comfortable refuge of the vast burrow. But the older Hannah is resolute:

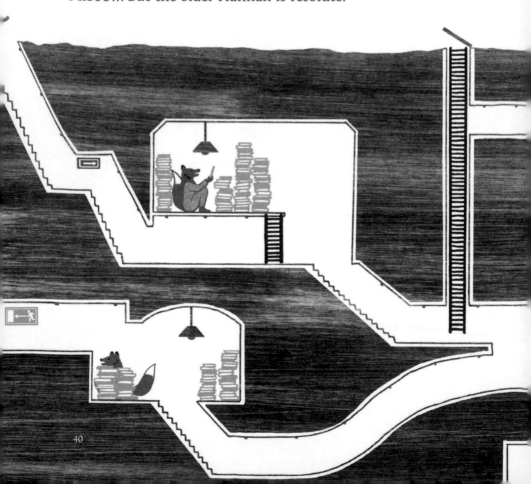

"We are not burrow thinkers," she reaffirms, "but field thinkers."
"Which involves the risk of being devoured," placidly comments
the fox as he closes the single eye he had bothered to open.
"This is true," admits the older Hannah. "But a life without risks
is no life at all, wouldn't you agree?"

On this note, the older Hannah takes her leave. She is sure
the young Hannah will follow her. And she is right.

Trying to follow the labyrinth of tunnels to the surface, the girl understands the insidious danger threatening them: "You see," sighs the exasperated older Hannah, "if thoughts are nothing more than words, we might very well end up lost… What is the good of digging tunnels if none of them lead to the world in which human affairs are played out!"

Nevertheless, after a thousand dead ends, the labyrinth finally comes to an opening. The two Hannahs resume their walk through the thick forest.
"Over there, a clearing," exclaims the young Hannah joyfully. Finally, a new stage!

Both Hannahs hasten their pace to reach the clearing.
Before emerging from the edge of the forest, the young Hannah looks around with worried eyes: no wolf to be seen… Whew! She can finally relax!
"Look, there is even a table and some chairs where we can have a rest!"
The girl skips happily into the clearing, but the older Hannah does not seem at ease.
"Come on," the girl beckons, "the wolf is not here, there is nothing to worry about!"
"Yet what if the furniture harbors a danger greater than the most vicious animal?"

All of a sudden, men emerge from the woods and come towards the clearing. One of them approaches the girl and fastens a label on her coat.

The older Hannah intervenes: "What are you doing?" she asks. And she crosses her arms so she can't be labeled as well.

"It's a simple formality," responds the man before taking a seat behind a desk. The other men take their seats as well. And each time a man sits down, another little Hannah appears on the other side of their desk.

"Now we are a multitude," murmurs the young Hannah as she looks about her, alarmed.

This clearing suddenly seems much less inviting than the forest she had just left. The line of little Hannahs starts to march, stopping in front of each desk where a man fastens a label, then shuffles and stamps papers here and there. Mesmerized by this new and unfamiliar scene, the young Hannah follows along in line.

As the slow line marches on, the older Hannah seeks a way
to escape towards the forest. When the line gets close to the
edge of the woods, she grabs the stiff hand of the mechanically-
marching child and pulls her behind a tree.

The young Hannah cries out: her hands as well as her legs
have turned to wood! The older Hannah vehemently rips off
the label that the man had fastened to the girl's coat. Then she
takes the child's hands and warms them for a long while.
"The office-men were getting ready to turn you into a puppet..."

Hidden behind the tree, the two Hannahs watch the
long line move along in the clearing of the office-men:
"Do they want to kill us?" asks the girl.
"It's worse than that, my dear Hannah. They are eliminating
the very principle of humanity. And they manage so well
that they themselves are no longer human: look closely,
they are also turning into wooden puppets!"
"Their minds as well, I bet!"

And now all the little Hannahs have become puppets
along with the bureaucrats.
"With the mind of a marionette and a head of wood,
one can no longer think," remarks the older Hannah.
"And the absence of thought is more dangerous than all
bad instincts put together…"

"But wait a minute!" exclaims the child. "If they are puppets, then someone must be pulling the strings from behind the scenes!"

And so both Hannahs slide along the edge of the trees in search of the puppet master.

Upon their arrival at the other side of the stage, they discover a huge pile of wood. The office-men are leading the puppet parade of little Hannahs to this pile.
"What is going to happen?" asks the girl with rising anxiety.
"Humanity is going to go up in smoke – the humanity of those who are going to be burned and of those who light the fire."

The young Hannah feels her throat tighten.
But her friend smiles at her and whispers:
"Think of the infinite possibility of new beginnings…"
And so she begins a race against the clock with
the puppet master.

Suddenly, the two Hannahs hear a high-pitched voice:
"Hey there gals, are you looking for me?"
They look up and see, on a branch overhanging the stage,
a strange character they can barely recognize.
"Those are the wolf's eyes," observes the girl.
"But he is strangely civilized," notes the older Hannah.
"That is somewhat reassuring," comments the girl.
"On the contrary, it is deeply disturbing," objects the
older Hannah. "As long as the wolf remains a wolf,
he can be kept on a leash. But if he becomes human,
he will infiltrate himself into the very heart of humanity."

But the man with the big eyes becomes impatient:
"Are you speaking about me? You are looking for
the puppet master, are you not? Well, here I am,"
he declares as he comes down from his branch to join
the two Hannahs. "Do you like my three-piece suit?
I find the jacket to be a perfect fit..."
"Stop all this!" screams the young Hannah, beside herself.
"Cut loose the puppet strings and give them back their
freedom! Prevent the office-men from lighting the pyre!"

The man with the wolf's eyes bursts out laughing:
"But I do not hold the strings, charming child! That is
what is so perfectly delightful. With their minds of wood,
my marionettes are incapable of telling the difference
between right and wrong, and they have flawlessly executed
my new law. You shall not kill, is that what you said earlier?
And well, as for me, I say: You shall kill! We stamped that
on paper, it made a new law, and it is engraved in the minds
of my little wooden puppets! Brilliant, don't you think?"

"I hate your new civilized style!" retorts the older Hannah.
"My dear lady," bows the man-wolf, "thank you for the
compliment."

The young Hannah yanks on the older one's sleeve.
"Look!" she says through tears.
In the middle of the stage, the pyre has been lit. As the two
Hannahs arrive on the scene, the pile of puppets is already
consumed and the executioners have disappeared. The child
despairs.

The fox, passing by, measures the damage. He scratches his head, embarrassed:

"I beg your pardon, my dear Hannahs, I've never really been interested in politics... I think it would be better if I returned to my burrow, don't you?"

"It is the trap of the burrow," replies the older Hannah.

"This is what happens if one refuses to enter the political scene..."

The fox disappears into a tunnel under the stage with his tail between his legs.

Do you **not** see a shadow trying to blend into the depths
of the forest?

"There is an office-man left!" exclaims the young Hannah.
She runs after the puppet and grabs him by the arm.
"Why did you do that?"
"I don't know! I am only a puppet, I followed the flow."
"You are lying: no string forced you to perform such acts."
"I obeyed the law," he clarifies as he removes a pile of papers
from a desk to justify himself. The older Hannah gives him
a disgusted look:
"And so you cannot speak for yourself? Not a single word that
was not put in your mouth? You are so appallingly trite!"

The young Hannah, desperate, turns to the older:
"How can a wooden puppet be judged?" she asks her.
"This is a big problem! But to judge also means to listen to
the person being judged. If we give him a voice, we force him
to speak for himself. When the words are just, they do more
than speak: they act."

As if on cue, the trees crumple one by one. The vegetation
quickly recedes. The forest fades bit by bit.

Men enter the scene and handcuff the office-man.
"You can judge me," he challenges, "but know that I was in
an unfortunate situation. I simply obeyed bad laws."
"This is what happens when one stops thinking and lets oneself
drift into the comfort of merely functioning... How can a public
space be built with men who know nothing but how to obey?"
"Give me another chance ... Give me another leader, a leader
with good laws, and I will obey just as well!"

"Your stupidity is revolting!" retorts the older Hannah.
"A citizen is expected to recognize as leader a person who
enforces good laws!"
"If you say so, I admit that my leader had bad laws. But he
was great!" declares the office-man with a glint of admiration
in his eyes. "See for yourselves: He managed to lift himself to
the highest level of society. From a mangy wolf, he became
the puppet master of the world. That is why I obeyed him."
"That is exactly the problem: you obeyed. As for political
obedience, it is not the same as schoolchild obedience.
In politics, obedience and support are one and the same."
"It is for this reason that you must leave the stage of human
affairs!" concludes the young Hannah.

And the office-man leaves the stage.

The two Hannahs find themselves alone on the stage which is still covered in forest moss.

"How did that happen?" moans the young Hannah.

"It happened. But it didn't happen everywhere. That is enough for this planet to remain livable for humanity."

"But will it still be livable tomorrow?"

The older Hannah smiles. The young Hannah and she share the same concerns.

"I have faith in the unforeseeable," replies the older Hannah. "And most of all, I have faith in you! In your opinion, who guarantees that the world has an ongoing chance for new beginnings?"

The girl thinks it over. Then her eyes light up with a new radiance: "Children do!"

"Exactly! The perpetual arrival into the world of strangers who will do things differently. Let's hope they are stubborn and endearing children…"

And so the young Hannah rolls up her sleeves.
"Stubborn and persevering," muses the older Hannah,
touched by the girl's determination.
"Are you going to help me build a new scene or not?"
the child asks. "I need your help to continue telling the story."

But new characters emerge from the wings to join her.
The older Hannah steps aside to let them pass.

"Oh, you know..." she says mischievously. "Those who transform the world into the theater of their audacity do not need help from someone who invents words..."

With these words, Hannah Arendt discreetly leaves the stage. She threads her way through the red velvet seats and pushes open the theater doors. She glances down at her watch: how time flies! She must get back to her apartment in a hurry: she has friends coming over for dinner tonight and has yet to prepare something to eat...

On the evening of December 4, 1975, such a very cold evening, Hannah Arendt gets up to serve coffee to her guests. She starts to say something but feels the weight of a heavy curtain fall upon her life. For her, the time for speech is over. She collapses into her armchair and takes her leave.

At the moment of her death, Hannah has the impression that a child who looks just like her is deciphering over her shoulder the book that she will never finish. Then she hears a little voice ring crystal-clear in her ear: "It would have been a shame to have put the final period on the life of the spirit!"

For Hannah is a palindrome. It is a name that can be read from left to right or from right to left. Then once you get to the H at the beginning, you can read right back to the H at the end. And so on and so forth until you no longer can tell if the end is not in fact a new beginning.

French edition
Marion Muller-Colard & Clémence Pollet
Le petit théâtre de Hannah Arendt
Design: Yohanna Nguyen and Avril de Perthuis
© Les petits Platons, Paris 2014

First edition
ISBN 978-3-03734-590-0
© diaphanes, Zurich-Berlin 2016

www.platoandco.net
www.diaphanes.com

Layout: 2edit, Zurich
Printed and bound in Germany